RECORD-BREAKING DINOSAURS

Written by Rosie Rowntree

Illustrated by Marina Halak

First published in 2026 by Hungry Tomato Ltd
F15, Old Bakery Studios, Blewetts Wharf, Malpas Road, Truro, Cornwall,
TR1 1QH, UK.

A CIP catalog record for this book is available from the British Library.

ISBN 9781835696644

Manufactured in the USA

Discover more at
www.hungrytomato.com

CONTENTS

Words in **BOLD** can be found in the glossary.

THE WORLD OF DINOSAURS

Get ready to explore the wonderful world of dinosaurs! From the tiny Confuciusornis to the giant Patagotitan, there are so many different types of dinosaurs to discover.

WHAT WERE THE DINOSAURS?

Dinosaurs were a group of **reptiles** that lived on Earth millions upon millions of years ago. They ranged in size from the bird-sized Archaeopteryx to the plane-sized Mamenchisaurus. The word "dinosaur" comes from two Greek words meaning "terrible" and "lizard".

WHEN DID THE DINOSAURS LIVE?

Dinosaurs lived on Earth for almost 180 million years. But they didn't all live at the same time! Some were around later than others. Scientists think that the earliest dinosaurs first appeared over 245 million years ago, while the last roamed the Earth 66 million years ago.

WHAT HAPPENED TO THE DINOSAURS?

66 million years ago, a large **asteroid** hit Earth at incredibly high speed. It caused a lot of fires and sent huge waves crashing across the land. Dust from the asteroid affected the weather and reduced the amount of food that the dinosaurs had to eat.

This made most dinosaurs become **extinct** – except for those that could fly, which survived and developed into the birds that we are familiar with today!

WHAT ARE FOSSILS?

Fossils are the remains of animals and plants that have been preserved for millions of years. They have been found on all seven of Earth's **continents**! Fossils of a dinosaur's entire **skeleton** are very rare. But even if they are found in bits and pieces, fossils allow scientists to learn a lot about the dinosaurs and their lives!

TYPES OF DINOSAURS

Scientists have arranged the dinosaurs into different categories based on things that they had in common, like their size or the way that they walked.

THEROPODS

Theropods all walked on two legs. Smaller theropods often had feathers, while larger ones were some of the biggest meat-eaters ever!

PACHYCEPHALOSAURS

These dinosaurs also walked on two legs. They are best known, however, for having very tough skulls!

CERATOPSIANS

These plant-eating dinosaurs had large eye-catching frills on their heads that could be used for protection. Their frills also helped them to keep warm in cold weather.

ORNITHOPODS

Ornithopods included several dinosaurs with duck-like beaks and crests on their heads. They were all plant-eaters rather than meat-eaters.

SAUROPODS

Sauropods included some of the largest dinosaurs to ever walk the Earth! They are easy to identify because they all had very long necks and tails, with incredibly small heads in comparison.

STEGOSAURS

Stegosaurs walked on four legs. Their most iconic features are the incredibly tough plates that ran across their backs and provided them with protection.

ANKYLOSAURS

Like stegosaurs, ankylosaurs had protective plates across their bodies. Ankylosaurs, however, had much shorter legs and often had tails that were shaped like clubs.

PTEROSAURS

These reptiles were close cousins of the dinosaurs and were the first animals after insects to develop the ability to fly. The very biggest had a similar wingspan to a small plane!

RECORD-BREAKING DINOSAURS

Some dinosaurs were born to break records. These incredible creatures pushed the limits of nature using their strength, size, and speed. Whether they soared through the skies at breakneck speeds or prowled across the land on massive legs, the dinosaurs in this book have all gone down in history!

Megalosaurus

When Megalosaurus was first discovered, scientists thought it was a large lizard because no one knew what dinosaurs were yet! That's why its name simply means "great lizard". It was the first dinosaur to ever be named.

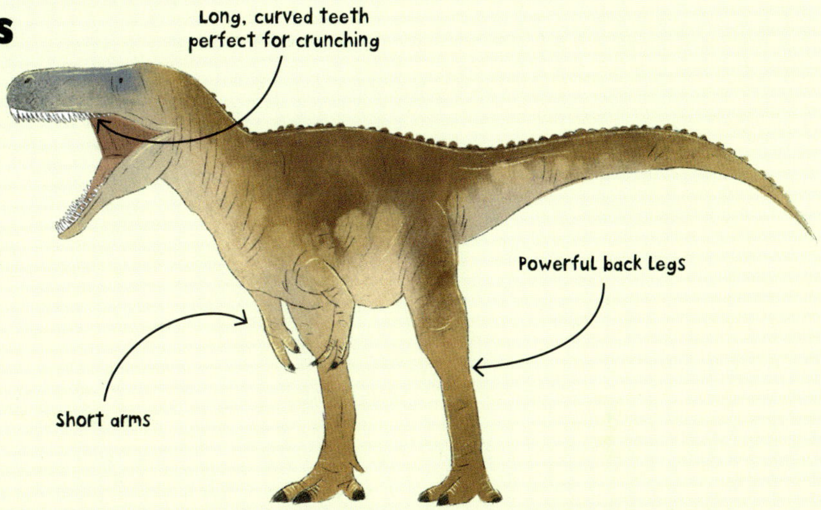

PRONUNCIATION: MEG-ah-low-sore-us

DIET: **Carnivore**

TIME PERIOD: Mid **Jurassic**

SIZE

SPEED

DEADLY RATING

Procompsognathus

This speedy dinosaur was the smallest dinosaur ever found at the time – although even smaller ones have been found since. It hunted **prey** like insects and small **mammals** using clawed hands that were relatively big compared to the rest of its body.

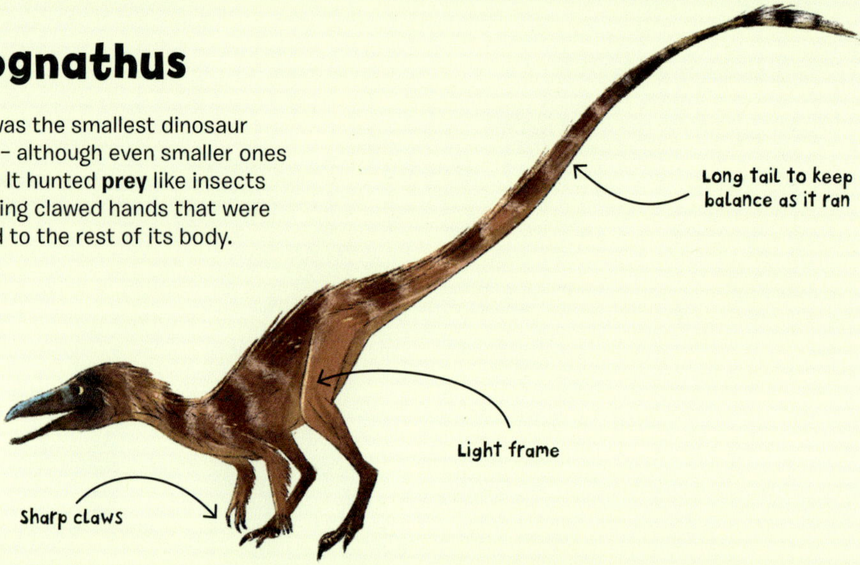

PRONUNCIATION: pro-comp-sog-NAY-thus	**SIZE**	1 of 5				
DIET: Carnivore	**SPEED**	4 of 5				
TIME PERIOD: Late **Triassic**	**DEADLY RATING**	2 of 5				

Brachiosaurus

The huge Brachiosaurus had very upright posture, preferring to hold its neck high in the air rather than out in front of it. It had a tiny head and an even tinier brain, and would have needed to spend most of the day eating just to get enough energy to survive.

PRONUNCIATION: BRAK-ee-oh-sore-us	**SIZE**	5 of 5
DIET: Herbivore	**SPEED**	2 of 5
TIME PERIOD: Late Jurassic	**DEADLY RATING**	2 of 5

Diplodocus

This dinosaur was one of the longest of all, thanks to its incredible neck and tail. Its neck allowed it to eat **vegetation** high above the ground in the **prehistoric** treetops, while its tail could be whipped from side to side to fend off **predators**.

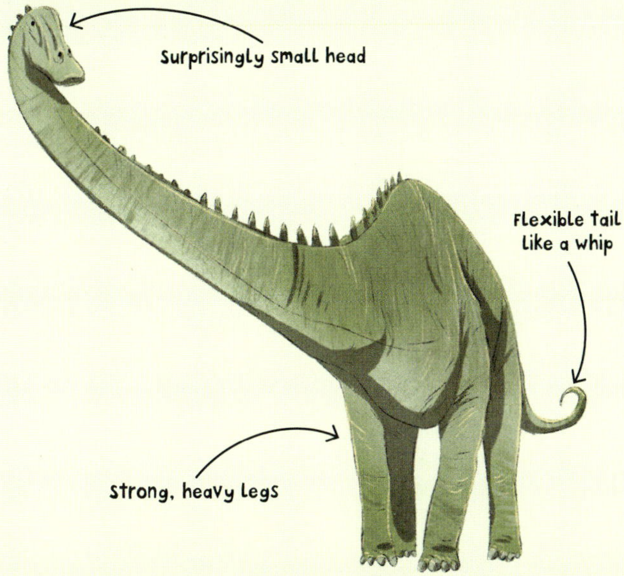

PRONUNCIATION: dih-PLOD-uh-kus	**SIZE** 5/5
DIET: Herbivore	**SPEED** 2/5
TIME PERIOD: Late Jurassic	**DEADLY RATING** 2/5

Quetzalcoatlus

Quetzalcoatlus is the largest flying animal of all time! It was the size of a giraffe, but that didn't stop it from leaping into the air and beating its massive wings to take off into the skies. It flew above rivers and oceans in search of fish and other small marine creatures to eat.

PRONUNCIATION: ket-suhl-kow-AT-luhs	**SIZE** 4/5
DIET: Carnivore	**SPEED** 5/5
TIME PERIOD: Late **Cretaceous**	**DEADLY RATING** 4/5

Because of the shape of its head and mouth, scientists initially thought Oculudentavis was a bird!

Oculudentavis

Even though its name means "eye-tooth-bird", scientists now believe that this creature was more like a lizard. It was extremely small and was the same size as a modern-day hummingbird. It had very big eyes and lots of teeth!

PRONUNCIATION: oh-cue-lu-den-TAH-viss	**SIZE** ●○○○○
DIET: Carnivore	**SPEED** ●●●○○
TIME PERIOD: Late Cretaceous	**DEADLY RATING** ●●○○○

Argentinosaurus

Argentinosaurus is one of the largest land animals to ever walk the Earth! It used its long neck to feast on plants that most other dinosaurs could not reach. But because of its sheer size, it was very slow. It had to rely on its bulk being enough to scare off any predators.

PRONUNCIATION: AR-gen-TEE-no-SORE-us

DIET: Herbivore

TIME PERIOD: Late Cretaceous

SIZE

SPEED

DEADLY RATING

Gallimimus

The speedy Gallimimus was over twice as fast as the average human. Having its eyes positioned more on the side of its head gave it a wide field of vision and meant it could spot any predators trying to sneak up on it, and sprint away before they could strike.

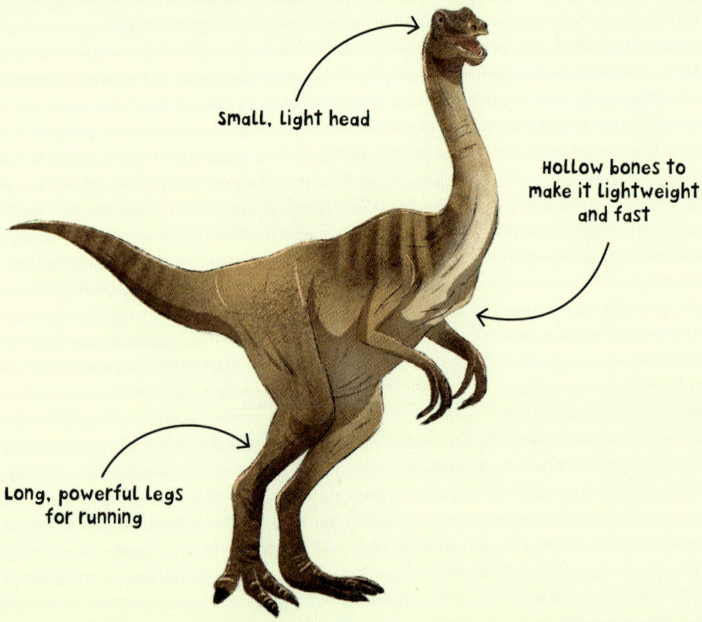

PRONUNCIATION: galley-MIME-us

DIET: Omnivore

TIME PERIOD: Late Cretaceous

SIZE

SPEED

DEADLY RATING

Vectaerovenator

Vectaerovenator possessed sharp claws and strong back legs. Large air spaces were found in its bones, which suggested it would have had a very light skeleton that made it nimble and **agile**.

PRONUNCIATION: vect-air-OH-ven-AH-tor	**SIZE** 3/5
DIET: Carnivore	**SPEED** 3/5
TIME PERIOD: Early Cretaceous	**DEADLY RATING** 3/5

Oryctodromeus

The unusual Oryctodromeus is the only known burrowing dinosaur! It dug its way underground using its sharp claws to create dens to shelter in during the winter, and to hide from predators.

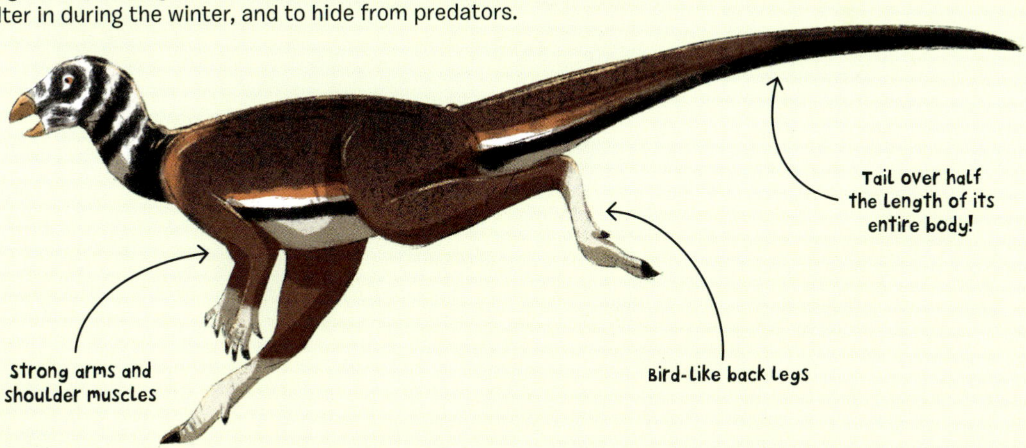

PRONUNCIATION: or-IK-tow-DROHM-ee-us	**SIZE** 2/5
DIET: Herbivore	**SPEED** 4/5
TIME PERIOD: Late Cretaceous	**DEADLY RATING** 2/5

Eoraptor

Eoraptor is one of the oldest known dinosaurs. It was relatively small – about the same size as a medium-sized dog – and walked on its back legs. It took advantage of having hollow bones to chase quickly after its prey.

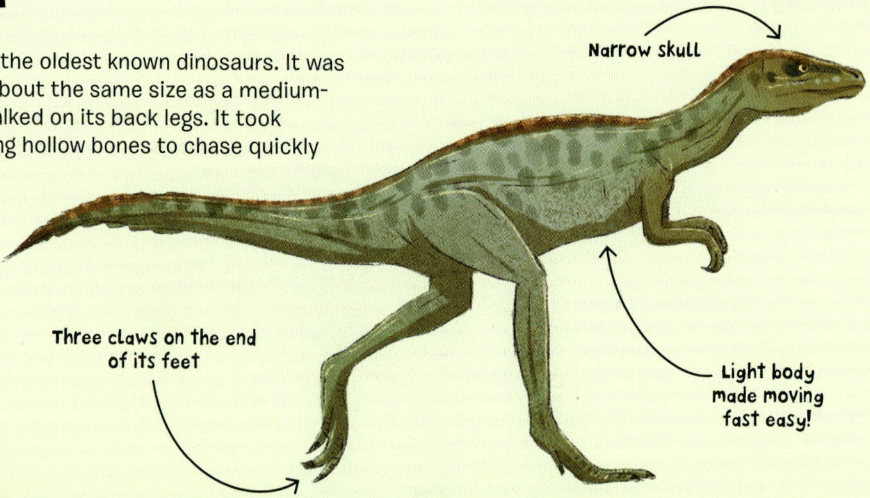

PRONUNCIATION: EE-oh-RAP-tor

DIET: Carnivore

TIME PERIOD: Late Triassic

SIZE

SPEED

DEADLY RATING

Herrerasaurus

Herrerasaurus was likely one of the first dinosaurs to roam the Earth. It pinned down its prey with its talons, opening its jaws very wide to use its backward-curving teeth to tear at skin and bone.

PRONUNCIATION: herr-ray-rah-SORE-us	**SIZE** ●●○○○
DIET: Carnivore	**SPEED** ●●●○○
TIME PERIOD: Late Triassic	**DEADLY RATING** ●●●○○

Mamenchisaurus

Mamenchisaurus had the longest neck relative to its body size of any dinosaur. It was five times longer than a giraffe's neck, and as long as a bus! Mamenchisaurus needed to have a very large heart to be able to pump blood all the way up to its head.

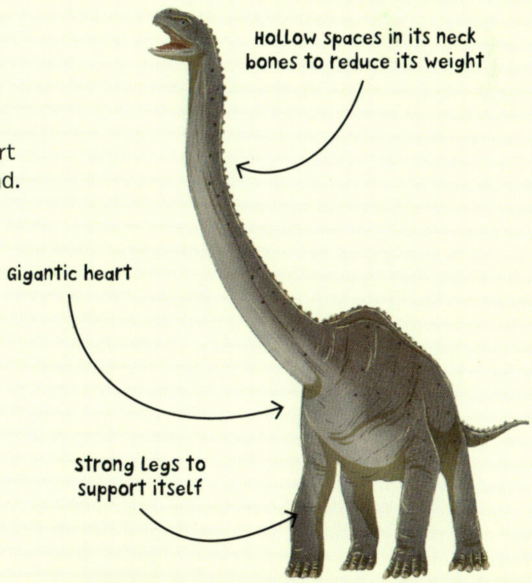

PRONUNCIATION: mah-men-chi-SORE-us	**SIZE** ●●●●●
DIET: Herbivore	**SPEED** ●○○○○
TIME PERIOD: Late Jurassic	**DEADLY RATING** ●●○○○

Archaeopteryx

Archaeopteryx is described as the "missing link" between birds and dinosaurs. It had a small frame and feathered wings like a bird. But it also had sharp teeth and a bony tail like a dinosaur. It can teach scientists a lot about about how dinosaurs and the birds that live on Earth in the present day are related!

PRONUNCIATION: AR-kee-op-TE-rix		**SIZE**	●○○○○
DIET: Carnivore		**SPEED**	●●●○○
TIME PERIOD: Late Jurassic		**DEADLY RATING**	●●○○○

Sauroposeidon

The neck bones of this dinosaur were so large, they were mistaken for the trunks of prehistoric trees when they were first discovered! Each bone was the same size as a fridge, and its neck overall was only slightly shorter than Mamenchisaurus's (page 17).

PRONUNCIATION: saw-ro-poh-SIE-don		**SIZE**	●●●●●
DIET: Herbivore		**SPEED**	●○○○○
TIME PERIOD: Early Cretaceous		**DEADLY RATING**	●●○○○

Torosaurus

Scientists initially thought Torosaurus was just a fully-grown version of another dinosaur. They did look very similar! But Torosaurus is actually its own **species**, and had the largest skull of any land-based animal ever! It likely lived and roamed in groups for protection against predators.

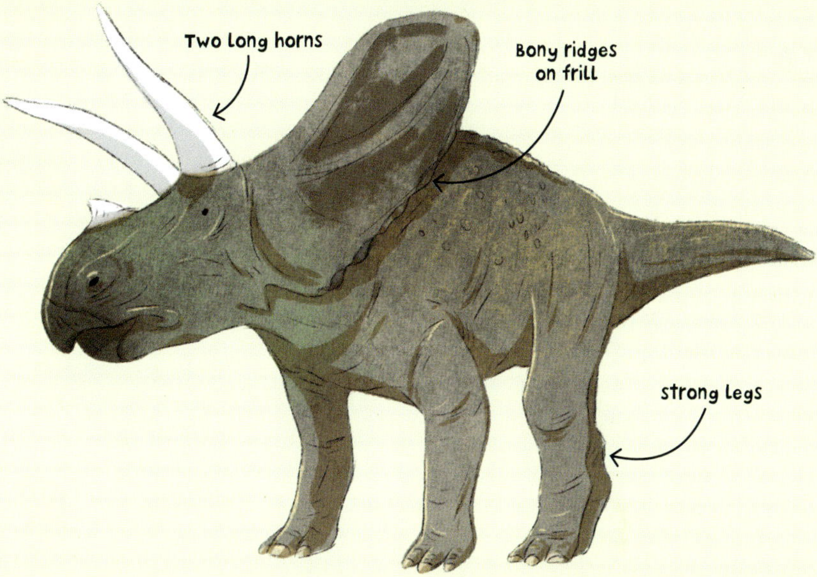

PRONUNCIATION: tor-oh-SORE-us	**SIZE** ●●●○○
DIET: Herbivore	**SPEED** ●●○○○
TIME PERIOD: Late Cretaceous	**DEADLY RATING** ●●○○○

Confuciusornis

Confuciusornis was a very small bird-like dinosaur, no bigger than a hardback book! It had strong, light, intricate feathers, including two very long ones that trailed out behind its tail. It is the earliest known creature of its kind.

PRONUNCIATION: kon-FEW-shus-or-niss	**SIZE** ●○○○○
DIET: Carnivore	**SPEED** ●●●○○
TIME PERIOD: Early Cretaceous	**DEADLY RATING** ●●○○○

Pteranodon

One of the largest flying reptiles ever discovered, Pteranodon had a huge wingspan that made it great at gliding. It soared through the skies above the oceans, with giant jaws like a pelican's that it could open wide and scoop up fish or other small marine creatures.

PRONUNCIATION: teh-ran-OH-don

DIET: Carnivore

TIME PERIOD: Late Cretaceous

SIZE

SPEED

DEADLY RATING

Alamosaurus

Despite having a small brain, Alamosaurus was still smart enough to know how to use its long neck to its advantage. It didn't waste energy moving its entire body from place to place in search of new food. Instead, it stayed in one spot and used its neck to reach places it hadn't yet eaten from.

PRONUNCIATION: ah-la-mow-SORE-us

DIET: Herbivore

TIME PERIOD: Late Cretaceous

SIZE

SPEED

DEADLY RATING

Chenanisaurus

Chenanisaurus is a very rare dinosaur, and is believed to be one of the last to roam the Earth! It existed at the same time as Tyrannosaurus rex and had a similar powerful bite with very small arms. However, the two lived on different continents and wouldn't have crossed paths.

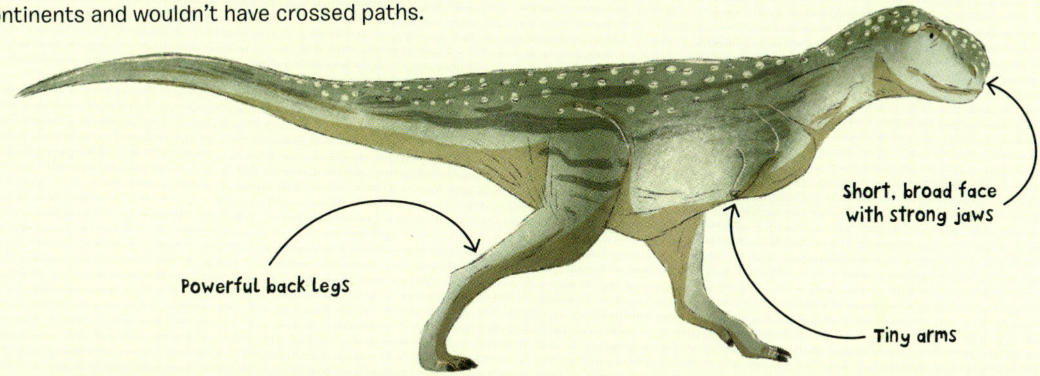

PRONUNCIATION: chen-an-ee-SORE-us

DIET: Carnivore

TIME PERIOD: Late Cretaceous

SIZE

SPEED

DEADLY RATING

Musankwa

Musankwa came from a group of plant-eating dinosaurs that all have small heads and long necks. While they were small to medium in size, scientists think that they later grew into the largest of all the land-based dinosaurs. Musankwa could teach us a lot about those giants!

PRONUNCIATION: MOO-san-kwah

DIET: Herbivore

TIME PERIOD: Late Triassic

SIZE

SPEED

DEADLY RATING

Yi Qi

Yi Qi was part of a group of dinosaurs that are closely related to modern-day birds. It had featherless wings and was capable of flying short distances between tree branches or gliding from those branches down to the ground. It was very, very small – only the size of a sparrow!

PRONUNCIATION: ee-key	**SIZE**
DIET: Insectivore	**SPEED**
TIME PERIOD: Mid Jurassic	**DEADLY RATING**

Eocarcharia

Eocarcharia had what looked like a bony eyebrow above each eye and had incredible blade-like teeth. These teeth would have made it a deadly opponent in a battle – no wonder it was one of the top predators of its day!

PRONUNCIATION: ee-oh-car-CAR-ee-ah	**SIZE**
DIET: Carnivore	**SPEED**
TIME PERIOD: Early Cretaceous	**DEADLY RATING**

Patagotitan

Patagotitan may have been the same length as the incredibly long Diplodocus (page 11), but it was also twice as tall and over three times as heavy! It was one of the largest dinosaurs ever to walk the Earth.

PRONUNCIATION: pat-ah-go-TIE-tan	**SIZE** ●●●●●
DIET: Herbivore	**SPEED** ●○○○○
TIME PERIOD: Early Cretaceous	**DEADLY RATING** ●●○○○

Pendraig

With a name that means "chief dragon", it may be easy to picture Pendraig as a big, heavy dinosaur. But no, it was actually the size of a chicken! It was still a good hunter though, and preyed on small reptiles using its sharp teeth and talons.

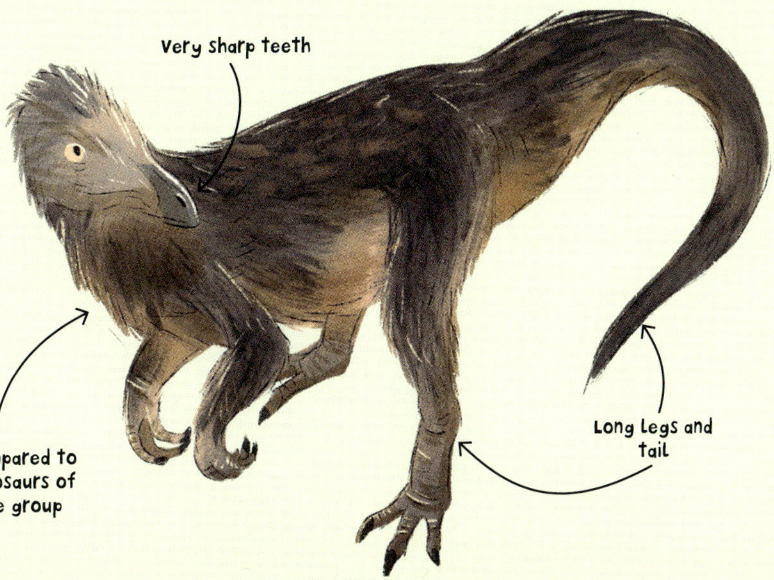

PRONUNCIATION: PEN-dray-g	**SIZE** ●○○○○
DIET: Carnivore	**SPEED** ●●○○○
TIME PERIOD: Late Triassic	**DEADLY RATING** ●●○○○

DID YOU KNOW?

What more is there to know about these record-breaking dinos? Let's take a look at some amazing facts and find out!

Despite its name, Megalosaurus is not the largest dinosaur ever discovered. The largest carnivorous dinosaur is the Spinosaurus.

Because of its long neck, scientists have suggested that Diplodocus might have had multiple hearts in its neck so that it didn't get too dizzy.

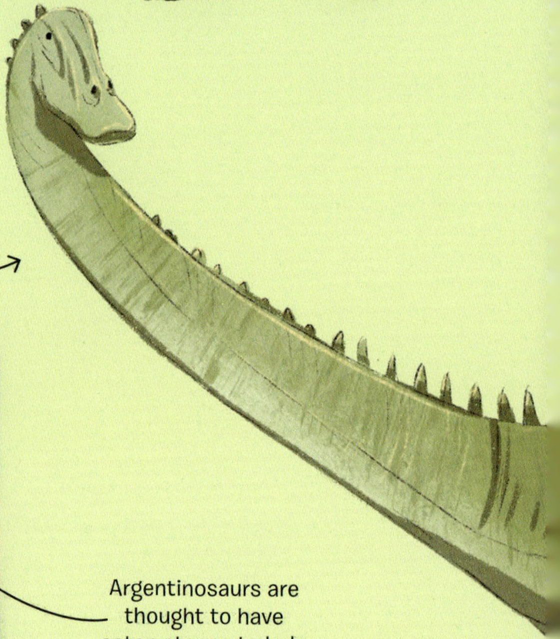

Argentinosaurs are thought to have eaten stones to help them digest plants.

Gallimimus didn't have teeth!

Herrerasaurus could open its mouth much wider than any other dinosaur of its size, making it a fierce opponent in battle.

Pteranodon is often mistaken for a dinosaur, but it was a pterosaur, a different type of reptile that lived alongside dinosaurs.

DINO DISCOVERY!

Want to be a dino detective? Paleontologists dig up clues to learn about dinosaurs - and you can too!

What is a Paleontologist?

A paleontologist is a scientist who looks for fossils, which could be old bones, teeth, and even footprints left behind by dinosaurs millions of years ago!

They dig very carefully so they don't break anything. Then, they study the fossils to figure out what dinosaurs looked like, how they lived, and what they ate.

Fieldwork: **Digging for Dinosaurs**

Paleontologists go out into deserts, rocky cliffs, and dry places where dinosaur bones might be hiding under the ground. These trips are called fieldwork.

They use small tools, like brushes and picks, to dig. When they find something, they wrap the fossil to protect it. Some fossils are so big, they need a truck or even a helicopter to move them!

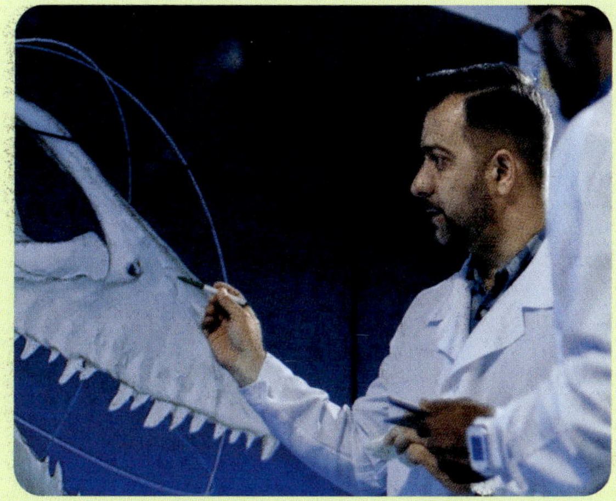

Lab Work:
Studying the Clues

Back in the lab, fossils are cleaned, measured, and sometimes scanned with special machines. Scientists study every detail to learn how the dinosaur moved, what it ate, or how it grew.

They might even use computers to make 3D models of the bones. This helps them look inside the fossils without breaking them.

Is It a New Dinosaur?

Some fossils don't match anything scientists have seen before. That might mean it's a new species! To find out, paleontologists compare the new fossil to other known bones. They look at its shape, size, and features.

Discovery

Fossils don't always come in one piece. Sometimes scientists only find part of a skeleton, like a leg or a jawbone. They use other fossils and guesswork to figure out how the bones fit together. That's how we get the giant dinosaur displays you see today!

WHICH RECORD-BREAKER IS THIS?

Follow the clues to uncover which record-breaking dinosaur you're thinking of! Start at the top and use YES or NO to follow the path.

START HERE

Was this dinosaur one of the biggest to ever walk the Earth?

YES – Was its neck really long?

- **YES** – Did it have a long and whip-like tail?
  - **YES** – IT'S A DIPLODOCUS
  - **NO** – IT'S AN ARGENTINOSAURUS
- **NO** – Did it have long front legs and hold its neck high like a giraffe?
  - **YES** – IT'S A BRACHIOSAURUS
  - **NO** – IT'S AN ALAMOSAURUS

NO – Was this dinosaur tiny, maybe even smaller than a chicken?

- **NO** –
- **YES** – Does it have feathers and might have glided or flown?
  - **YES** –
  - **NO** – IT'S AN EORAPTOR

IT'S AN EORAPTOR

IT'S A DIPLODOCUS

IT'S AN ARGENTINOSAURUS

IT'S A BRACHIOSAURUS

IT'S AN ALAMOSAURUS

PICK A DINOSAUR!

Choose one of the following dinosaurs - now, answer the questions to find them!

Eoraptor
(page 16)

Chenanisaurus
(page 21)

Eocarcharia
(page 22)

Gallimimus
(page 14)

Archaeopteryx
(page 18)

Alamosaurus
(page 20)

Argentinosaurus
(page 14)

Diplodocus
(page 11)

Brachiosaurus
(page 10)

Confuciusornis
(page 19)

Was it built for speed, like an ostrich or emu?

YES

IT'S A GALLIMIMUS

NO

Did it have sharp teeth and live near the ocean?

YES

IT'S A CHENANISAURUS

NO

IT'S A EOCARCHARIA

Did it have a long tail and claws like a raptor, but also have wings?

NO

IT'S AN CONFUCIUSORNIS

YES

IT'S A ARCHAEOPTERYX

GLOSSARY

Agile – the ability to move very quickly and easily.

Asteroid – small, rocky objects that orbit the Sun.

Carnivore – an animal that only eats meat.

Continents – huge pieces of land on Earth. For example, Africa and North America are separate continents.

Cretaceous – a period of time that lasted from about 143 to 66 million years ago.

Extinct – a species (see right) of animals with no living members.

Fossils – the remains or impression of plants and animals that lived long ago.

Herbivore – an animal that only eats plants.

Hollow – something that has an empty space inside.

Insectivore – an animal that only eats insects.

Jurassic – a period of time that lasted from about 201 to 143 million years ago.

Mammals – warm-blooded animals (including humans) that produce milk to feed their young.

Omnivore – an animal that eats both plants and meat.

Predators – animals that hunt and kill other animals for food.

Prehistoric – the time before humans existed.

Prey – an animal that is hunted by other animals for food.

Reptiles – a group of cold-blooded animals, including snakes, lizards, crocodiles, and some types of dinosaurs.

Skeleton – the bony frame that supports and protects the body of a person or animal.

Species – a group of living things that share characteristics and features, and can produce young with each other. For example, Stegosaurus and Triceratops are different dinosaur species.

Triassic – a period of time that lasted from about 251 to 201 million years ago.

Vegetation – plant life in a particular area.

INDEX

ABOUT THE AUTHOR

Rosie Rowntree is a children's author living in the west of Cornwall. Sharing her love of learning through her writing, she is passionate about sparking curiosity in children as they begin to broaden their horizons and learn about their surroundings - and beyond!

ABOUT THE ILLUSTRATOR

Marina Halak is a talented illustrator of children's books from Ukraine. Her stunning illustrations are inspired by her own childhood, children, nature, magical moments and fairy tales. Marina is also the illustrator behind the related series, *Dogs* and *Cats*.

Picture Credits:
(abbreviations: t=top, b=bottom, m=middle, l=left, r=right)

Additional illustrator: Tjarda Borsboom 26-27bm.

Shutterstock: Catmando 25tl (gallimimus); Dotted Yeti 25tl (scenery); Elenarts 24tr; Esteban De Armas (25br); Frame Stock Footage 27tl; Gorodenkoff 26mr; Kamomeen 24tl; Rijk van de Kaa 27mr; Warpaint 24bl.

Every effort has been made to trace the copyright holders, and we apologize in advance for any unintentional omissions. We would be pleased to insert the appropriate acknowledgments in any subsequent edition of this publication.